BIOINDICATOR SPECIES

DRAGONFLIES
MATTER

by Tammy Gagne

Peachtree

Content Consultant
Ruud Schilder, PhD
Assistant Professor of Entomology & Biology
Penn State University

Core Library

An Imprint of Abdo Publishing
abdopublishing.com

abdopublishing.com

Published by Abdo Publishing, a division of ABDO, PO Box 398166, Minneapolis, Minnesota 55439. Copyright © 2016 by Abdo Consulting Group, Inc. International copyrights reserved in all countries. No part of this book may be reproduced in any form without written permission from the publisher. Core Library™ is a trademark and logo of Abdo Publishing.

Printed in the United States of America, North Mankato, Minnesota
072015
012016

Cover Photo: Martin Fowler/Shutterstock Images
Interior Photos: Martin Fowler/Shutterstock Images, 1; Rob Hainer/Shutterstock Images, 4; iStockphoto, 6, 16, 18, 20, 22 (top right), 22 (left center), 22 (bottom left), 22 (bottom right), 43; Shutterstock Images, 8, 34; Dorling Kindersley Universal Images Group/Newscom, 10; Red Line Editorial, 12; Darko Vojinovic/AP Images, 14; Andrew Howe/iStockphoto, 22 (top left); Vitalii Hulai/iStockphoto, 22 (center); Ingram Publishing/Newscom, 24; Joel Sartore/National Geographic Creative/Corbis, 26; Mitsuhiko Imamori/Minden Pictures/Corbis, 28; Stephen Morton/AP Images, 30; Gerald Herbert/AP Images, 32, 45; Joe Blossom/NHPA/Photoshot/Newscom, 36; Tony Kyriacou/REX/Newscom, 38

Editor: Jon Westmark
Series Designer: Laura Polzin

Library of Congress Control Number: 2015945397

Cataloging-in-Publication Data
Gagne, Tammy.
 Dragonflies matter / Tammy Gagne.
   p. cm. -- (Bioindicator species)
ISBN 978-1-68078-010-9 (lib. bdg.)
Includes bibliographical references and index.
1. Dragonflies--Juvenile literature. 2. Dragonfly ecology--Juvenile literature.   3. Environmental protection--Juvenile literature.   I. Title.
595.7--dc23

                                                    2015945397

CONTENTS

CHAPTER ONE

MUCH TO TELL

A blue dasher dragonfly takes off over a pond. It flies after a mosquito above the water. The dragonfly rises and falls as it darts through the air. Morning dew shimmers on the insect's four clear wings. Its deep-blue body reflects off the calm water.

Dragonflies spend most of their lives in or near water. Most female dragonflies lay their eggs in a marsh, pond, or other waterway. Young dragonflies

Scientists estimate dragonflies have lived on Earth for more than 250 million years.

Female dragonflies carefully choose where to lay their eggs.

are called larvae or nymphs. They stay in the water after they hatch. Like fish, larvae breathe through gills. As adults, dragonflies take to the air. But they stay near water to find food and to mate.

Changes in water conditions can have a big effect on dragonflies. A change in water temperature can change how quickly dragonflies grow. Poor water quality can affect how many dragonfly larvae survive. In this way, dragonflies are bioindicators. Biodindicators are animals scientists study to learn more about the health of an ecosystem. When dragonflies are doing poorly, other plants and animals in the ecosystem are likely also suffering.

Flashy Fliers

Dragonflies are found on every continent on Earth except Antarctica. There are more than 3,000 different species. These long-winged insects come in every color of the rainbow. Many people admire dragonflies' beauty. But there is a lot more to dragonflies than their stunning looks.

Dragonflies can beat their wings 30 times per second.

Dragonflies are talented fliers. They can fly straight up or down, forward or backward. They can even hover. Adult dragonflies catch all their prey while flying. But being a great flyer has a downside. If a dragonfly is hurt or unable to fly, it will starve.

Dragonflies do not start out flying. In fact they spend most of their time in the water when they are young. Larvae spend a long time growing and shedding their skins underwater. Finally they emerge and shed their skins one last time. Then they take to the air. Dragonflies may spend up to four years as larvae but just a few months as adults.

Threats to Dragonflies

Poor water quality is a major threat to a number of dragonfly species. In order for dragonflies to grow into adults, they must live in oxygen-rich water. Adult dragonflies breathe air. But larvae get their oxygen from the water. Pollution can lower oxygen levels in water. This is because bacteria use oxygen to break down pollutants. High levels

Natural Pest Control

Dragonflies play a big role in controlling mosquito populations. Many people find these biting insects annoying. And mosquitos are known to spread diseases. But they make up a large part of the dragonfly's diet. A single adult dragonfly can eat hundreds of mosquitoes in one day. Without dragonflies, mosquito populations would grow hugely.

Dragonfly larvae come in many different shapes and sizes.

of pollution can force bacteria to use up too much oxygen. A lack of oxygen can be particularly bad for dragonflies. As larvae, some species sit burrowed in the ground, waiting for prey to swim by. This is the first place to be affected by low levels of oxygen.

Larvae that hunt in this way may die if pollution is high.

A decrease in dragonflies is one of the first signs an ecosystem is in trouble. Animals such as tadpoles, fish, and insects need high-quality water. Dragonflies rely on these animals for food. And larger predators, such as birds and frogs, eat dragonflies.

Soon after dragonflies begin to die, other animals become affected. This is because dragonflies are both predators and prey. Without dragonflies

PERSPECTIVES
Hands-Off Parents

Some animals have a small number of offspring. With many of these species, females lay eggs or give birth and then help their young grow into adults. Dragonflies take a different approach. They lay many eggs and leave them to develop on their own. Since larvae and adults live in different habitats, there is little adults can do to help the larvae. Dragonflies lay hundreds or thousands of eggs to help ensure some of the offspring will become adults and reproduce. Many young dragonflies do not make it past the first week of adulthood. Recently emerged dragonflies are weak and unable to fly. This makes them easy prey.

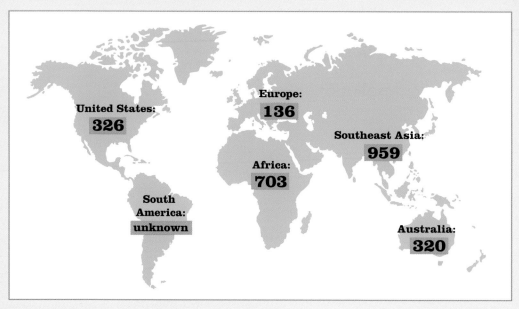

Dragonfly Species by Region
When it comes to dragonfly species, not all parts of the world are equal. Warmer areas, including Southeast Asia and Africa, have more species than the colder regions have. No one knows how many dragonfly species live in South America. Many unknown species could live in the depths of the Amazon rain forest, where humans have not yet explored. Why do you think more dragonflies live in warmer climates than in colder ones?

the balance of an ecosystem becomes disrupted. All living things in an ecosystem depend on one another.

Dragonflies thrive in many parts of the world. Nearly all species of dragonflies in the United States are plentiful. In other places, though, species are in trouble. For example, many types of dragonflies struggle to survive in the United Kingdom. Bog pools where the white-faced darter lives are drying out, ruining the animal's habitat. Rising sea levels and increased salt in the water are hurting the Norfolk hawker. By studying these and other problems facing dragonflies, people can learn about changes occurring in the environment.

EXPLORE ONLINE

The website below discusses dragonflies as bioindicators. How does the information compare with what you have read in Chapter One? Write a paragraph about what dragonflies can tell humans about the environment. Use facts to back up your opinion.

Dragonflies and the Environment
mycorelibrary.com/dragonflies-matter

CHAPTER TWO

ON THE DECLINE

Many dragonfly populations have had a big drop in recent years. For instance, one-fifth of the dragonflies around the Mediterranean Sea are threatened. One-third are threatened in the United Kingdom. There are many reasons for the declining number of dragonflies around the world. Most of these factors are connected to human actions.

Pollution is one way in which humans can endanger dragonflies.

Shrinking wetlands can make it hard for dragonflies to reach adulthood.

Habitat Loss

Habitat loss is one reason dragonfly populations are down. Dragonflies need plenty of water to stay healthy and reproduce. New farming methods help farmers save water. But the practices limit where dragonflies can live and lay their eggs.

In the past, farmers in Cambodia and other parts of Asia flooded rice fields until harvest time. This practice gave dragonflies plenty of water to use. But it created water shortages for people. New ways of farming have cut water usage in Asia in half. This change means dragonflies have fewer places to lay their eggs. It also means that dragonfly larvae have less living space. They must compete for food with other insects. This results in fewer dragonflies living to adulthood. And it means fewer dragonflies are mating and continuing the species.

Having fewer dragonflies nearby is bad for crops. Farmers in poorer countries, such as Madagascar, rely on these insect-eaters as a natural way of controlling

Pesticides spread through the air can make their way into dragonflies' water habitats.

pests. When dragonflies are present, the number of pests eating farmers' crops is much lower.

Pollution

Dragonflies help cut the number of pests feeding on farmers' crops. But they do not get rid of the pests completely. In an effort to protect their crops, many farmers use pesticides to keep the remaining insects away. These chemicals are sprayed on the plants, but they do not stay there. The chemicals can travel long distances.

Wind can sweep pesticides through the air. When rain falls, the chemicals may be washed to nearby streams. Even if there are no large bodies of water close to the crops, pesticides soak through the soil into groundwater. The chemicals spread faster once they reach water.

As the chemicals build up in the water, they sicken dragonflies. In the most polluted areas, dragonflies die as a result. The dragonflies that survive leave the area in search of a new habitat. When this happens, females often lay fewer eggs.

Governments consider the dangers of pesticides when they

First Warning

Only one dragonfly species is endangered in the United States. The state of Illinois listed the Hine's emerald dragonfly as endangered in 1991. This was the first sign the species was in trouble. Its declining numbers were a sign the species' ecosystem was in danger as well. One of the biggest reasons for the Hine's emerald dragonfly's decline was pollution in wetlands. In 1995 the US government also listed the Hine's emerald dragonfly as endangered.

Carbon dioxide released into the air can contribute to a warming climate.

make laws about use of the chemicals. In some cases, farmers use more pesticides than the law allows. But studies have shown that even allowable amounts of some pesticides may hurt both the world's waters and wildlife.

Climate Change

Dragonflies are sensitive to changes in temperature. As a result, climate change is a big threat to them.

One part of climate change is the slow rise of Earth's temperature. This is caused by greenhouse gases released into the atmosphere. These gases trap the sun's heat, causing the air to warm slowly. People release greenhouse gases, such as carbon dioxide, when they burn fuels. These fuels include oil, coal, and gasoline.

Dragonflies cannot produce their own body heat. For this reason they prefer warm climates. Some species migrate to warmer areas as seasons change. In very warm places, dragonflies must protect themselves from overheating. On sunny

PERSPECTIVES
Waiting Out Droughts

Dragonflies help people learn how global warming affects ecosystems. But some dragonfly species have adapted to survive temperature changes. Water can dry up due to rising temperatures. When this happens, certain dragonfly larvae burrow into the earth to reach damper ground. They may remain underground for years. When the conditions aboveground improve, the dragonflies return and complete their life cycles.

Everything Is Connected
One of the reasons dragonflies are bioindicators is they serve as both predators and prey. This diagram shows some of the relationships of a dragonfly larva. The arrows show the flow of energy through the ecosystem. If dragonflies were to disappear from an area, how would other species be affected?

days, this means finding shade and being less active. Dragonflies hunt most at dusk when the air is cool and other insects are on the move. Rising temperatures, though, mean this cooler time of day is gradually becoming warmer and warmer. When the air becomes too hot, dragonflies may leave one area in search of a cooler one.

Before 1996 the red-eyed damselfly did not live in the United Kingdom. The species is now found throughout the southern half of England. Higher temperatures drove it from mainland Europe to the United Kingdom. Damselflies are very similar to dragonflies. Migrations like this may keep some species from dying out. But such moves can have negative effects on the species' original ecosystems. Insect populations go up when dragonflies leave. Many insects carry diseases. More insects can increase the spread of disease.

Relocation also increases competition in the new location. Dragonflies must compete with other populations of dragonflies for food.

Studies have shown that warmer air is hurting 14 of the 39 dragonfly species in the United Kingdom.

Dragonflies prefer warm climates. But conditions that are too warm can force populations to move elsewhere.

Dragonflies do best when conditions are just right. If temperatures continue rising, species now living in the United Kingdom could move to other places. This would continue the cycle of upsetting ecosystems.

Dragonflies can move easily from one place to another. But most animal species cannot. Not all animals have wings to help them travel long distances. Many water species can migrate only if the waterway where they live flows into another one. The fact that some dragonflies are migrating shows climate change may soon put other animals at risk.

FURTHER EVIDENCE

Chapter Two focuses on the reasons many dragonfly species are decreasing in population. Visit the website below. Find a quote that supports this chapter's main idea. Is this evidence the same as what you have read in the chapter? What new information does it offer?

Dragonflies and Damselflies: Order Odonata
mycorelibrary.com/dragonflies-matter

CHAPTER THREE

WHY DRAGONFLIES MATTER

Many dragonfly species face serious threats. These threats are not only bad for dragonflies. Losing dragonflies can bring harm to many other species, including humans. This is one of the main reasons scientists study dragonflies. They want to know how issues affecting dragonflies' surroundings affect other species.

A group of boys in Mozambique help collect dragonflies for a research study.

Dragonfly larvae need clean water to survive until adulthood.

Water Quality

Poor water quality drives dragonflies from their habitats and affects their entire ecosystem. People are largely to blame for the problem. Humans drain Earth's wetlands to make room for more homes and businesses. The human population is growing quickly. And people need places to live and work.

Destroying wetlands hurts more than just dragonflies and the other animals that live in these areas. Wetlands are helpful to the world. As rainwater runs into wetlands, they take out nutrients, sediment, and waste from the water before it reaches bigger bodies of water. In this way, wetlands help clean Earth's water.

Without wetlands, people may suffer along with wetland animals. Wetlands store water when severe rainstorms hit. Without wetlands, crops and other land would flood. Wetlands even put food on people's tables and create jobs for fishers. Nearly all the fish

PERSPECTIVES
The Hunter and the Hunted

Some people see dragonflies as pests. As larvae they eat just about any animal smaller than they are. They even eat some things that are bigger. Tadpoles, fish, and other dragonflies are all fair game. People who keep outdoor fishponds often find that dragonflies eat their newly hatched fish. But fish that survive into adulthood often eat dragonflies.

Studying dragonflies can teach humans about issues in the environment.

and shellfish caught in the southeastern United States come from wetlands.

Learning Lessons

Many years ago, coal miners used canaries to check if the air was safe inside the mines where they worked. These birds can sense if carbon monoxide is in the air. Carbon monoxide is a dangerous gas that is both colorless and odorless. If the birds stopped singing, it was unsafe for people to work in the area.

Dragonflies and other bioindicators can serve a similar role to canaries. The difference is dragonflies give humans information on a much bigger scale. They can tell if there are problems with Earth's environment. Where pollution is hurting the dragonflies, it can also harm other animals and people.

Making a Change

Dragonflies are not the only animals suffering because of pollution and climate change. These things affect many other

One Dragonfly Species, Two Continents

The globe skimmer dragonfly lays its eggs in temporary freshwater pools fed by rainwater. This means the species must follow the rains to reproduce. The globe skimmer has the longest migration of any insect. It travels across the Indian Ocean, from India to Africa and back. The total distance is approximately 11,000 miles (17,703 km). This journey means the globe skimmer needs healthy ecosystems on two continents to survive.

An oil-covered dragonfly rests on marsh grass after an oil spill.

species and their ecosystems. But when people work to save dragonflies, the benefit multiplies. Other animals, humans, and the environment share it.

Many people dislike small insects. But Ellen Sousa of the Ecological Landscape Alliance suggests getting rid of insects can cause more problems than it solves. She said in an interview:

> When we spray the pests, we also wipe out their predators. When it comes to insecticides, the pests will almost always make a comeback before the predators do, so instead of developing even more toxic sprays to control pests, we should concentrate on supplying more habitat for their natural controllers. So although there are many hardy non-native plants that are wildlife-friendly in some way, I encourage the planting of regional natives wherever possible as the simplest way to support the widest variety of the insects that in turn support the birds, bats, dragonflies, and the other animals . . . . If we want to preserve our remaining biodiversity, we need to provide wildlife with what they need, because we all rely on the ecosystem services they provide.

Source: Ecological Landscape Alliance. "Spotlight on Native Habitat Gardens: An Interview with Ellen Sousa." ELA. Ecological Landscape Alliance, September 14, 2012. Web. Accessed June 1, 2015.

What's the Big Idea?

What is the main idea of this passage? What evidence does the author use to support her points? Find two or three sentences that show how she backed up her opinions.

CHAPTER FOUR

WHAT WILL HAPPEN NEXT?

Saving the world's dragonflies is important for many reasons. As long as these incredible insects exist, they will give people insight into the health of other living things. By saving dragonflies, humans protect Earth itself.

Education

The first step to saving any threatened or endangered species is creating awareness about the problem.

By working to fix issues facing dragonflies, humans also help other animals.

A guide speaks with visitors at the Norfolk Wildlife Trust in Norfolk, United Kingdom.

Organizations such as the British Dragonfly Society work to tell people about the decreasing numbers of dragonfly species. The group publishes a magazine called *Dragonfly News* for this purpose. The organization believes if more people know dragonflies are in trouble, the insects stand a greater chance of survival.

Larger environmental groups, such as the World Wildlife Fund and the Sierra Club, help focus people's attention on the problems the environment is facing. In this way, these groups act as a voice for dragonflies. When people take steps to save the environment, they are helping dragonflies at the same time.

Conservation

One of the best ways to help save dragonflies is conservation. By preventing wetlands from being destroyed, people protect dragonfly habitats. Researchers have seen dragonfly populations increase in nature reserves around the world. And they have seen the return of species that had left the area.

In 2007 the British Dragonfly Society offered kids remote-controlled toys for helping to locate a rare species.

In 2001 a rare species called the white-faced darter reappeared in Cumbria, England. In 2013 a species thought to be extinct reappeared in Wadi Wurayah National Park in the United Arab Emirates. This species, called *Urothemis thomasi*, had not been seen since 1957. The species is so rare it does not yet have a common name.

Every person can make a difference for dragonflies and for the environment by taking simple steps. Using less electricity, for instance, lessens the amount of pollution in the environment. Most electrical plants produce large amounts of carbon dioxide. When people use less electricity, the plants release less of this damaging gas. Donating money to wetland conservation groups is also another way to make a difference.

Research

The state of Illinois is helping dragonflies by funding research about them. It has donated approximately $6 million to help scientists study the endangered Hine's emerald dragonfly. The University of South Dakota also has helped this endangered animal.

Research projects are a key part of saving the world's dragonflies.

PERSPECTIVES
A Natural Approach

Sometimes small changes can have big results. Some companies sell dragonflies as pest control for gardeners and farmers. These companies are helping dragonflies in two ways. First, they are increasing dragonfly populations. Second, they are lessening the amount of pesticides the gardeners use. This move helps create a safer environment for both dragonflies and the other animals that share their habitats.

Slow Down!

One of the biggest threats to the Hine's emerald dragonfly is people driving too fast. Studies have shown that cars kill approximately 3,300 of these dragonflies each year in Door County, Wisconsin. But only fast-moving cars kill them. The dragonflies often survive when they are hit by slow-moving cars. Researchers have suggested lowering the speed limit in the area to 35 miles per hour (56 km/h) to help save the species.

By studying the insects and tracking their populations, researchers can accomplish two goals. First, they use the data these bioindicators provide about the world around them. Second, they learn how people can make changes to save both the dragonflies and the planet.

The world still has much to learn about how to keep dragonflies and the environment out of danger. If people do not pay attention to signals from these species, the problems will get worse before they get better. Whether or not they can be solved depends on how long humans take to respond.

A 2009 report from the International Union for the Conservation of Nature talked about the importance of dragonflies and how the public can help:

> *Dragonflies are excellent tools for freshwater conservation because: They are useful for providing a first insight into the quality and structure of aquatic habitats. Their distribution can be mapped with the aid of volunteers, so that much more information is available for this group than for any other. They are generally popular and have a wide audience, and thus can be used as appreciated ambassadors for freshwater conservation, which is important for raising awareness among non-specialists.*
>
> *In order to use dragonflies as a quality indicator, up-to-date information on distribution is needed. For specific projects, specialists can gather information, however, to obtain countrywide information it is far more cost-efficient to establish a network of volunteers.*
>
> Source: Elisa Riservato, et al. "The Status and Distribution of Butterflies of the Mediterranean Basin." IUCN Red List. IUCN Centre for Mediterranean Cooperation, March 16, 2010. Web. Accessed June 1, 2015.

Consider Your Audience

This passage was written to for government officials. Rewrite this passage for volunteers. How is the new version different?

Common Name: Dragonfly

Scientific Name: *Anisoptera*

Average Wingspan: 3 to 5 inches (7.6 to 12.7 cm)

Average Weight: 0.0001 ounces (0.003 g)

Color: Varies by species

Average Life Span: A few months to a few years as larvae, but only a few months as adults

Diet: Insects, such as mosquitoes, and their larvae

Habitat: Waterways on every continent, except Antarctica

Predators: Birds, fish, and frogs

What's Happening: Many dragonfly populations are decreasing.

Where It's Happening: Various regions around the world

Why It's Happening: People are polluting the world's waterways.

Why It's Important: The decreasing dragonfly population is a sign the environment is in trouble.

What You Can Do:

- Write a letter to your state representative. Explain the importance of dragonflies as bioindicators.
- Conserve energy every day, and encourage others to do so as well.
- Donate money to an environmental organization that works to protect dragonflies.

Say What?

Learning about bioindicators can mean learning a lot of new vocabulary. Find five words in this book you have never seen or heard before. Use a dictionary to find out what they mean. Using your own ideas, write down the meaning of each word. Then use each word in a new sentence.

You Are There

Close your eyes, and imagine you are hiking in the woods. You come upon a pond where hundreds of dragonflies are darting through the air above the water. Describe what else you might see in this area. What can you tell about the overall health of the ecosystem?

Tell the Tale

Write 200 words from the point of view of a dragonfly forced to leave its habitat in search of clean water. Make sure to set the scene, develop a sequence of events, and include a conclusion.

Take a Stand

What do you think is the best way to spread the word about the threats dragonflies and the environment are facing? Write a letter to someone you think can help make a difference, such as a politician or a celebrity. Urge that person to help educate others on the topic of bioindicators and what they reveal about the planet's future.

GLOSSARY

biodiversity
the variety of plant and animal species in a specific environment

conservation
the preservation and protection of a plant, animal, or habitat

endangered
at great risk of extinction

extinct
no longer existing

insecticide
a chemical used to kill insects

larvae
the young, wormlike forms of insects that hatch from the eggs of many species

pesticide
a substance used to kill pests

predator
an animal that kills and eats other animals

sediment
material carried by water

threatened
at risk of extinction, just short of being considered endangered

LEARN MORE

Books

Basher, Simon. *Climate Change: A Hot Topic*. London: Kingfisher, 2015.

Earley, Chris. *Dragonflies*. Richmond Hill, ON: Firefly Books, 2013.

Simon, Seymour. *Global Warming*. New York: HarperCollins, 2013.

Websites

To learn more about Bioindicator Species, visit **www.abdopublishing.com**. These links are routinely monitored and updated to provide the most current information available.

Visit **mycorelibrary.com** for free additional tools for additional tools for teachers and students.

INDEX

ABOUT THE AUTHOR

Tammy Gagne is the author of more than 100 books for adults and children. She resides in northern New England with her husband and son. One of her favorite pastimes is visiting schools to speak to kids about writing.